Plenty Good Room

A BIBLE STUDY BASED ON AFRICAN AMERICAN SPIRITUALS

LEWIS V. BALDWIN

Abingdon Press / Nashville

PLENTY GOOD ROOM: A BIBLE STUDY BASED ON AFRICAN AMERICAN SPIRITUALS
STUDENT BOOK

Copyright © 2002 by Abingdon Press

This book is printed on acid-free, elemental-chlorine-free paper.

Library of Congress Cataloging-in-Publication Data

ISBN 0-687-05033-2

02 03 04 05 06 07 08 09 10 11—10 9 8 7 6 5 4 3 2 1

MANUFACTURED IN THE UNITED STATES OF AMERICA

Contents

Introduction

African American spirituals have been called the earliest sacred music of the United States. Although it is difficult to determine exactly when spirituals were created, historians agree that the birth of the spirituals coincided with the emerging days of slavery. Thousands of spirituals originated during the time of slavery and, remarkably, these songs have been passed down from generation to generation.

The origin of the spirituals was influenced by many factors. First, slaves brought melodies, rhythms, and tones of music from their West African culture. This music was complex in beat, meter, and syncopation. The style also called for emotional improvisation, feeling, and expression in song.

Second, slaves were exposed to Christianity. Although they came to accept the same religion professed by the larger society, slaves were able to transcend some of the theological interpretations given to them, thereby grasping deep, spiritual truths.

Third, after combining musical form with words from the Bible and doctrines of the Christian faith, slaves added their own experience. Slaves in the United States experienced a horrible form of bondage and servitude. Although slavery is an ancient institution, slaves who came to the United States, to a degree not known in earlier times, were degraded, abused, and tortured for economic and political profit. The horror that the slaves endured seems almost unimaginable in contemporary times, and yet slavery in the

> "And even when the white preacher tried to convince the African slave that the God of the Bible is a God who requires the slaves to be obedient to their masters and subservient to the white people, the slaves heard the call of God for justice, equality, and freedom."
>
> —William McClain, *Come Sunday: The Liturgy of Zion* (1990)

United States is embedded firmly in our history. Remarkably while the slaves suffered tremendous affliction and oppression, they were able to create exquisite songs of beauty, inspired by the power of God and the yearning for freedom. These songs, used by the slaves for comfort, encouragement, and healing, have now been bequeathed to us.

Slaves brought the African cultural tradition of applying music to every situation, from work routines to the naming of children. Every aspect of life was commemorated by song. Throughout history, this music has been called by many names, including jubilees, folk songs, shout songs, sorrow songs, slave songs, slave melo-dies, minstrel songs, and religious songs. And yet, because of the fervent passion and religious emotion of the songs, they became most commonly known as spirituals. The power of God's Holy Spirit, resonating with the spirits of all who sang them, created a notable intensity that often led to joyous shouts. Slaves were able to worship in the midst of their busy days by singing these songs, even when they were forbidden to attend church. Sung alone or in a group, the spirituals' power to heal, to soothe, and to strengthen made the music's impact a powerful testimony.

> "These songs are prayers, praises, and sermons. [Slaves] sang them at work; in leisure moments; they crooned them to their babies in the cradles; to their wayward children; they sang them to their sick, wracked with pain on beds of affliction; they sang them over their dead."
>
> —John Wesley Work
> *Folk Songs of the American Negro* (1974)

> *I'm gonna sing when the Spirit says sing,*
> *I'm gonna sing when the Spirit says sing,*
> *I'm gonna sing when the Spirit says sing,*
> *And obey the Spirit of the Lord.*

The world is indebted to the slaves, incredible, faith-filled saints, who survived this devastating period in history. These saints left behind music that has inspired millions, including the freedom fighters of the Civil Rights Movement in the 1960s. Like the generations before us, we are encouraged to pass on this beautiful, spirit-filled music to our descendants.

Plenty Good Room: A Bible Study Based on African American Spirituals includes six spirituals: "Rock-a My Soul," "Go Down, Moses," "Balm in Gilead," "Ain't Dat Good News," "Every Time I Feel the Spirit," and "Plenty Good Room." These songs were chosen for two reasons. First, each spiritual is relatively well-known and should be familiar to listeners, even those who may not have much exposure to them.

Second, the rich biblical content of each song provides the unique opportunity for participants to study Scripture along with the words of the songs. The biblical themes of all six spirituals move from the Hebrew Bible to the New Testament, covering God's message of liberation of a people, salvation offered by the atoning grace and mercy of Jesus Christ, and the dispensation of the Holy Spirit.

> In the 1860's and 1870's, African American college choirs preserved and popularized the spirituals. The tradition of touring choirs, quartets, and glee clubs emblazoned the Spirituals on the minds of the American public and increased the technique of choral or part-singing.
>
> —Cheryl A. Kirk-Duggan, *Exorcizing Evil*, (1997)

Plenty Good Room is not only the title of the study and the name of one of the spirituals used; it also reflects the injunction of Jesus in Luke 14:13: "When you give a banquet, invite the poor, the crippled, the lame, and the blind." In God's kingdom there is plenty good room for all, regardless of race, station, gender, or ethnicity. God's table is open to all, and all are welcome. In Luke 17:21, Jesus states: "The kingdom of God is among you." God's kingdom, in which there is plenty of good room, reflects not only heaven or the afterlife but also the present. As Christians striving to be obedient followers of Christ, we are reminded to make room for all persons, including ourselves, in the community of faith through acts of mercy, justice, and care. God's kingdom is willed on earth as it is in heaven.

Plenty Good Room: A Bible Study Based on African American Spirituals provides an opportunity to reflect on the history and the context of the spirituals' origins. The accompanying CD allows you to hear the songs' beautiful melodies and harmonies. Take the time to reflect on the sessions, the stories, the Bible readings, and the spirituals themselves in order to deepen your knowledge and understanding of the past and to hear the eternal truths of sacred word through song.

Session One

Luke 16:19-26

Key verse: "But Abraham said, 'Child, remember that during your lifetime you received your good things, and Lazarus in like manner evil things; but now he is comforted here, and you are in agony." (Luke 16:25).

"Rock-a My Soul"

Chorus:
Rock-a my soul in the bosom of Abraham
Rock-a my soul in the bosom of Abraham
Rock-a my soul in the bosom of Abraham
Oh, rock-a my soul

Rock-a my soul in the bosom of Abraham
Rock-a my soul in the bosom of Abraham
Rock-a my soul in the bosom of Abraham
Oh, rock-a my soul

Verse:
So high, you can't get over it
So low, you can't get under it
So wide, you can't get around it
Oh, rock-a my soul

Rock-a my soul in the bosom of Abraham
Rock-a my soul in the bosom of Abraham
Rock-a my soul in the bosom of Abraham
Oh, rock-a my soul (Repeat Verse)

Let's Listen: Holy Movement and Worship

"Rock-a My Soul" is a syncopated and rhythmic spiritual. One of the most notable aspects of the composition is the beat, which is solid and penetrating. Voices follow along with the beat, enunciating words with a syncopated flair. On the accompanying CD, a lilting, vibrating soprano solo carries the first verse, progressing down the musical line until there is a dramatic pause that ends, "Oh, Rock-a my soul!" After the chorus, a mellow tenor repeats the verse, and like the soprano, melts into other voices, reverently returning in unison to the vibrant, syncopated style of the chorus.

A song of jubilee, "Rock-a My Soul" calls for praise and worship. The enticing style makes liturgical expression and group interaction suitable for singers and listeners alike. Deep inside the rhythms is a delightful emotion that spreads like wildfire once the spiritual begins. Infectious beats and convincing melodies evoke a joyous worship style, one in which the slaves who sang and composed them must have delighted in offering up praise to God. The meter and rhythm of "Rock-a My Soul" make it perfect for group singing, movement, and interaction.

> ## How were spirituals composed?
>
> "[Folks just] makes [their] own verses, just naturally comes to us, and we make our own rhyme as we go."
>
> —Uncle Fil Hancock, ex-slave, 1934

The words and musical style of "Rock-a My Soul" demonstrate how slaves tried to make the best of their situation by worshiping God through music and community. Like many spirituals, "Rock-a My Soul" has a communal feel, calling for persons to sing the song together. It was one of many spirituals sung in the slave quarters, throughout the workdays or at secret brush harbor meetings in the woods. Often slaves had to sing quietly so the masters would not hear them.

Rock of One's Soul

"Rock-a My Soul" was also among the many spirituals that reflected the slaves' sense of self-worth in the face of an unjust system that questioned and violated their humanity. A major belief in society was that slaves had no souls; they were viewed as slightly above animals. In the minds of some slave owners and many others of European descent, this belief justified the slaves' subhuman treatment. Yet "Rock-a My Soul" explicitly proclaims that the slaves believed they did have souls, and furthermore,

> "The only [church] I knowed 'bout was when we'd git together in [the] night and have prayer meetin' and singin'. We [used] to go way out in [the] woods so [the] white folks [wouldn't] hear nothin'."
>
> —Stearlin Arriwin, ex-slave, 1935

that their souls were intimately connected to God. Jesus was the rock, the steady anchor in a stormy, wind-tossed land. They could hold on to Jesus, even in the worst of times; and this rock gave them comfort and strength. Slaves knew from deep inside their beings that within their souls was the life and vitality stemming from the presence of God's Spirit and that this Spirit moved within. This was a Spirit they could feel! One of the reasons worship was so popular with the slaves, even after days of hard, draining work, was that the activities of praise and worship confirmed that they were alive and connected to the Divine.

When they felt the movement of God within their souls, slaves were reassured that they were precious, that they were holy and sanctified persons, and that they were loved and adored by Jesus Christ. Their souls were "rocked" as they danced and worshiped, and their souls were comforted in "the bosom of Abraham." They received a taste of awesome majesty and divine power simply by singing this spiritual as they rocked back and forth, lifting up the name of the Most High God. No matter what the slave masters or anybody else said, slaves knew what they felt. They felt the Spirit of God. God was real to them.

The phrase "so high, you can't get over it" reflects the slaves' understanding of the love and the depth of God. To the slaves, God was taller and wider than any mountain. God was so high and wide that no one could get over or around him. God was so low that no one could get underneath him. The slaves understood God's love to be big, fat, wide, tall love, the kind of love that envelops all of creation with broad, sweeping affection.

When slaves sang "Rock-a my soul," they were singing about this great love. Such love was experienced and felt like a sensation tingling in the skin, traveling up the spine, jumping and twitching in the chest. Powerful, emotional love carried the slaves along with this spiritual; and singing about all this love (more than enough to spare) sent slaves dancing, jumping, and shouting.

God's love was so great that the slaves had to tell someone, even their masters. They could not keep this good news to themselves! Some slaves were not allowed to praise God openly, so they simply did so in secret, chanting in whispers about the awesome power of God's love. No matter what their situation, slaves had to sing; and "Rock-a My Soul" is a spiritual that calls for heartfelt expression.

The Alvin Ailey American Dance Theater, a ballet and dance troupe that has performed for over 19 million people in 67 countries since its founding in 1958, is best known for its thrilling numbers expressing black heritage. "Revelations" is the title of the troupe's signature performance. At the end of an entire program, the troupe often uses "Rock-a My Soul" as the musical background for this awe-inspiring and powerful presentation.

Read a Parable by Jesus: Luke 16:19-26

Jesus tells a colorful story, or parable, in which the experience of a rich man is contrasted with that of a poor beggar named Lazarus. Due to their economic stations in life, the two men had vastly different lifestyles. Lazarus lay outside the rich man's gate, begging for food and clothing. The rich man dressed in fine clothes and ate sumptuously. After both men died, judgment was served: The rich man was sent to torment in Hades. Lazarus, however, was given comfort in Abraham's bosom. Here, "Abraham's bosom" describes the world of comfort and peace—heaven—in the life after death.

It is interesting that in the parable Lazarus is named and the rich man goes nameless. Another interesting part of the parable is that the rich man, while tormented in hell, still expected Lazarus to serve him. However, Lazarus was protected by God's comfort, tucked away in Abraham's bosom. He did not have to suffer anymore. This relief from suffering was the hope of the slaves who longed to reach a place where they could be at peace.

Slaves and "Rock-a My Soul"

Slaves, upon hearing this parable, clearly identified with poor Lazarus and saw their slave masters as the uncaring rich man. Although in this world the slaves suffered physically and mentally from want while their masters lived in splendor, they believed that in the next world justice would be served and the order of things would be reversed. The slaves believed that, like Lazarus, after death they would be comforted in Abraham's bosom. The parable of Lazarus and the rich man demonstrates that divine justice cannot be reversed.

In light of the parable, "Rock-a My Soul" becomes a subtle criticism of slavery. Under the guise of the song, slaves could openly express themselves. Even when it was sung in the presence of slave owners, few of the whites were perceptive enough to look beyond the biblical roots of the song and its seemingly otherworldly dimension. Yet, clearly, this spiritual had political undertones for the slaves. "Rock-a My Soul" suggests that the slaves believed that the evils of this world should be reversed. Social and economic oppression is inherently wrong and disapproved of by God. This song demonstrates that many slaves believed that justice was due not only in heaven but also in this world. Slaves also believed that one day evil persons of the world would suffer for their sins, while poor and suffering persons would be rewarded. This is why the slaves could sing "Rock-a My Soul" with such joy and exuberance. They were looking forward to resting in Abraham's bosom in this life and throughout eternity.

The Origin and Destiny of Our Souls

Many of us in today's world often allow artificial barriers to separate some groups from others. Some remain isolated in their daily lives by turning increasingly to work, the Internet, or other means of technology. As people of faith, however, we are taught that all persons have common origins as children of God. In Luke 16:19-26, Lazarus needs the food that graces the rich man's table. Later, the rich man asked Lazarus to help him escape the torment of hell. Likewise, we are called to help our brothers and sisters.

Further, as "Rock-a My Soul" indicates, there is an important question posed to every Christian: While we all originated in the bosom of Abraham, will we ultimately find rest there when our journey here on earth has ended? Moreover, can we sing with joy and peace in our hearts now, even when we face difficulties and hardships in this life? "Rock-a My Soul" reminds us that despite suffering, poverty, headache, and strife, we have a God who loves us. This God loves us so much that we will be rocked into comfort by God's love, if only we reach for it.

FOOD FOR THOUGHT

1. How does reflecting on "Rock-a My Soul" honor the religious legacy of slaves? How can the legacy of the slaves be honored through praise and worship and the singing of this song?

2. What does the phrase "the bosom of Abraham" describe? Does it have the same meaning in Luke 16:19-26 as it does in the spiritual? What is the meaning of the word *soul*? How is it different from or similar to the meaning of the word *spirit*? What do you think it means for the soul to be "rocked"? How did such a message comfort the slaves? How can we be comforted today by such a message?

3. What does the story of Lazarus and the rich man tell us about the importance of overcoming barriers to human understanding, community, and cooperation? How would the rich man's life have been different if he had lived in a more faithful and loving way? What does the story tell us about societal injustice and inequities? Can Jesus' view on the subject be gleaned from the parable? How are we called to address these issues as followers of Jesus Christ?

4. How can the descendants of slaves and slave masters work to heal and reconcile the pain of the past while rediscovering our faith heritage? What can we learn from each other? How should we teach the lesson of forgiveness to our children?

13

Session Two

Exodus 3:1-10

Key verse: "Then the LORD said, 'I have observed the misery of my people who are in Egypt; I have heard their cry on account of their taskmasters. Indeed, I know their sufferings" (Exodus 3:7).

"Go Down, Moses"

Verse:
When Israel was in Egypt land:
Let my people go;
Oppressed so hard they could not stand,
Let my people go.

Chorus:
Go down, Moses,
'Way down in Egypt land,
Tell ole Pharaoh
To let my people go.

"Thus saith the Lord," bold Moses said,
Let my people go;
"If not, I'll smite your first-born dead,"
Let my people go. (Repeat Chorus)

Verse:
No more shall they in bondage toil,
Let my people go;
Let them come out with Egypt's spoil,
Let my people go. (Repeat Chrous)

Heart and Soul

"Go Down, Moses" is a soulful, plaintive spiritual. The tone is mournful and serious. With a slow tempo and a regular, pronounced beat, the spiritual is melancholy and intense. On the *Plenty Good Room* CD, male and female voices singing this song are rich and deep. Stylistically, each note is heavy, marked, and strong. Musical accompaniment on the piano matches the voices with a steady, accented background, coloring the melody line and enriching the striking harmonies among the soprano, alto, tenor, and bass lines. After the group sings the powerful refrain in unison, a soprano voice, seeming to weep, leads off the first verse. The second verse, sung by a bass,

14

is distinctive, authoritative, and commanding. All of the voices, which display added vibrato or a pulsating effect in the sound, reflect a depth of emotional concern and pity. The effect is strength and force in the sound, capturing the essence of divine concern for suffering people. Clearly, God's love and devotion, expressed through the style, tone, and character of this spiritual and demonstrated effectively by the impact of the singing voices, are depicted in "Go Down, Moses."

> When will Jehovah hear our cries?
> When will the sun of freedom rise?
> When will for us a Moses stand,
> And bring us out from Pharaoh's hand?
>
> —Daniel Coker
> *"Prayers From a Pilgrim's Journal"*
> (1820)

Escape and Deliverance From Slavery

"Go Down, Moses" is a spiritual with revolutionary content and meanings. The biblical references and the call for freedom were applied by the slaves to their own situation of living in bondage. Used as a musical code for slaves escaping on the Underground Railroad, "Go Down, Moses" was very important to the slave community because of its double meaning. Masters and other whites hearing the song were only impressed by the strong biblical themes. However, to escaping slaves and persons helping them along the way, this spiritual also represented hidden meanings, hints, messages, and signals.

With its forceful and somber mood, "Go Down, Moses" made a marked impression on slaves as they traveled through dangerous territory, hid in swamps from bounty hunters, and ran from wild animals. Runaway slaves typically traveled by foot at night and slept during the day. Often, slaves would hide in the homes or on the property of kind people who would provide them with food, clothing, and medical assistance. A large number of persons who aided slaves on the Underground Railroad were white and belonged to religious groups such as the Methodists and the Quakers. Houses and other places in which slaves were allowed to hide were called "stations" because they were the stops slaves would make while traveling on the "train." Singing this song must have helped to inspire the slaves with a sense of divine sanction for their escape. They believed that God wanted them to be free; and the holy, authoritative sound of the song encouraged that faith.

15

> Harriet Tubman was the most famous Underground Railroad conductor. She risked her life dozens of times, going into slave territory in order to help slaves escape. Her bravery helped to liberate over 300 men, women, and children from slavery. Because of her courage and sacrifice, she was nick-named Moses.

"Go Down, Moses" has been popularized throughout history by many famous performers. The African American artist Paul Robeson (1898–1976) sang the spiritual quite often during his stellar career. Civil Rights students and activists during the Sixties also sang "Go Down, Moses" while partici-pating in marches, protests, and sit-ins.

Quest for Freedom: Exodus 3:1-10

In this text Moses, while tending sheep, is encountered by God. Speaking through the form of a burning bush that was not consumed by fire, God called Moses by name and established a connection by noting Moses' her-itage as a child of Abraham. The presence of God's very being in the entire area made it imperative that Moses honor the site by removing his sandals.

Moses was commissioned to go to Egypt and confront Pharaoh in order to free the Israelites. The love and concern of God for the people was reflected in God's symbol of an unquenchable fire, a heart burning with compassion and solidarity with the people's sorrows in slavery. When the people cried to God, they were heard. God knew of the people's oppression and told Moses that God had "come down" to deliver the Israelites. God had resolved not only to deliver the people from slavery, but to bring them up into a fruitful land of their own. Moses, having been sent by God, went to lead the people out of bondage into their new territory.

The Slaves' Identification With the Israelites

The words and context of "Go Down, Moses" come directly from the Book of Exodus and demonstrate the slaves' familiarity with and enthusiasm for the Bible. However, according to state laws at the time, the majority of slaves were not allowed to learn to read. Those slaves who were allowed to attend white churches with their masters listened closely to sermons, remembered the Bible stories, and put them to song. In many of these white churches, as former slave Sarah Sanders Barclay reflected, "there was a place in the back...for slaves to sit."

Many slaves learned to read in secret. They were determined to learn, even if it was against the wishes of their masters and the law. Painstakingly, slaves taught themselves the alphabet from stolen books as they squatted in the fields between rows of cotton. At night in their cabins they read under faint candlelight or even by the light of the moon. Some slaves convinced their masters' children to teach them lessons out of schoolbooks. Others practiced with newspapers, advertisements, or anything they could find. However, the main book they wanted to read was the Bible.

> "It was the law that if a white man was caught [trying] to educate a [N]egro slave, he was liable to prosecution entailing a fine of fifty dollars and a jail sentence."
>
> —John W. Fields, 89-year-old former slave (1936)

Despite the many hardships they faced, some slaves actually became quite proficient at reading and writing although they had to hide these skills from their masters. Evidence of their learning can be found in their cultural legacy, which includes an oral and written heritage among which the spirituals are foremost.

The chorus of "Go Down, Moses" itself is a direct paraphrase of Exodus 3:10. Clearly, the slaves who composed the song understood the Bible story so intimately that the words indicate Moses' geographical location in the Sinai Peninsula requiring him to travel south, or "down" to Egypt. The verses of "Go Down, Moses" are also very specific to the setting of the Exodus text and thereby to the condition of the Israelites. The words of the first verse, "When Israel was in Egypt land \ oppressed so hard they could not stand," ring out poignantly when we consider the situation of the slaves. Such a description of oppression was meaningful because it was experienced in the real-life conditions of the slaves, thus making the Scripture come alive. Slaves were well acquainted with oppression and identified readily with the depictions of the Israelites' suffering.

> "My Uncle Ben...could read [the] Bible.... [The master took the] Bible 'way from Uncle Ben and say it put ...bad ideas in [his] head, but Uncle [got another] Bible and hides it and massa never finds it."
>
> —John Bates, former slave (1936)

By repeating the words of the Exodus text in the chorus, words of God that command Moses to tell Pharaoh to let "my people go," the slaves secretly expressed their belief that they were God's people, just as the

Israelites were. Despite their condition, the slaves did not believe they were chattel, possessions, or animals. Instead, they believed that they belonged to God and were created in God's image. The double meaning of "Go Down, Moses," with its biblical layering, allowed the slaves to worship openly with this powerful, yet dangerous theological interpretation, often without incurring the indignation and punishment of their masters.

Justice and Equality

"Go Down, Moses" indicates that slaves believed that God is on the side of the oppressed. This view continued to be held throughout the history of the African American community and was captured dramatically during the Civil Rights Movement. Freedom fighters in the 1960s sang and rewrote the words of many spirituals. By singing songs like "Go Down, Moses," they were strengthened and inspired to march, speak, sit-in, and stand up for civil rights throughout the United States. Striving for equality for all oppressed persons is viewed as an issue of freedom. Just as God loved the Israelites so much to demand their freedom, God demands the freedom and liberation of all suffering persons everywhere. By viewing themselves as the people of God, the slaves expressed their belief in the calling of God to be free.

Freedom Today

Today, people are still being called to serve God in the pursuit of freedom. Throughout church and society, there are various roles and responsibilities persons assume in order to promote equality and dignity for all. Some are called to be clergy persons or politicians. Others are called to be activists who challenge systems of social, economic, and political oppression. This is particularly important in the case of the poor, African Americans, immigrants, and other ethnic groups who suffer disproportionately from the oppressive forces of poverty and economic exploitation, police brutality, unjust court systems and sheer neglect in the United States. Because of this, the biblical theme of the Exodus, sparked by the beautiful, yet haunting melody of "Go Down, Moses," remains a powerful influence upon the African American community's sense of liberation and justice. We must continue to ask ourselves how this theme may be applied to increasing levels of understanding deliverance for all humankind today.

FOOD FOR THOUGHT

1. Why does God speak to Moses from a burning bush? It is suggested that the burning bush symbolizes the presence of God. What do you think?

2. How would the slaves have heard "Go Down, Moses?" What about later generations? In what ways do contemporary Christians interpret this spiritual?

3. What was God's plan of deliverance for the Israelites? How would you compare the experience of the Israelites under Pharaoh with that of the African American slaves under their slavemasters? How were the experiences the same? different?

4. How can we be certain that God is on the side of the oppressed? What does this mean for the Israelites? What did this mean for African American slaves? What does it mean for us today? Is the African American community still oppressed/enslaved today? How so?

5. Whom would you label the pharaohs in today's world? Are they merely the rich and powerful? Do they come in all races, ethnic backgrounds, and nationalities? How can we best deal with them? Are they part of God's plan of deliverance?

Session Three

Jeremiah 8:18-22

Key verse: "Is there no balm in Gilead? / Is there no physician there? / Why then has the health of my poor people / not been restored?" (Jeremiah 8:22).

"Balm in Gilead"

Chorus:
There is a balm in Gilead,
To make the wounded whole,
There is a balm in Gilead,
To heal the sin-sick soul.

Verse:
Sometimes I feel discouraged,
And think my work's in vain,
But then the Holy Spirit
Revives my soul again.
(Repeat Chorus)

Verse:
Don't ever feel discouraged,
For Jesus is your friend,
And if you look for knowledge,
He'll ne'er refuse to lend.
(Repeat Chorus)

Verse:
If you cannot preach like Peter,
If you cannot pray like Paul,
You can tell the love of Jesus,
And say "He died for all."
(Repeat Chorus)

Plaintive and Soothing Harmony

"Balm in Gilead" is extremely melodious, pleasing, and sweet to hear. On the *Plenty Good Room* CD, a calming and tranquil piano introduction prepares the listener to relax and enjoy. Flowing at a gentle, delicate, and almost delayed pace, this spiritual evokes the sensation of peace. The style is one of comfort and tranquility. Singing voices for this song are reassuring and loving with beautiful and memorable harmonies. Warm, soothing arms of sound envelop the listener, calming mind, body, and spirit. Since the beat is dramatically slow and easy, singers must extend the

> "Hope in the black spirituals is not a denial of history. Black hope accepts history, but believes that the historical is in motion, moving toward a divine fulfillment."
>
> —James H. Cone, *The Spirituals and the Blues* (1972)

notes at each level of pitch, sustaining the words. This conveys the spiritual's positive message. The tone is in a minor key; and this contributes to a lamenting, almost mournful sound. A feeling of powerful sadness evoked by the slow movement and harmonies makes this spiritual distinctive from some of the other lively slave songs. Despite its words of hope, "Balm in Gilead" can be called a "sorrow song" because of the melancholic cadence in the voices and musical accompaniment. Four-part harmony, with male and female parts, creates a light and airy, although profound, sound.

> "I [saw] slaves for sale on [the] auction block. They [sold them according to strength] and muscles. They [were] stripped to the [waist. I saw] the women and little [children crying and begging] not to be separated, but it didn't do no good. They had to go."
>
> —Stearlin Arriwine, ex-slave, 1936

Slavery's Balm for Weary Souls

"Balm in Gilead" ranks among the most popular spirituals during slavery times. Slaves often sang this song during secret prayer meetings at night in the woods. The soft, gentle melody made it easy to sing this song quietly without losing any of the moving effect. A song of comfort, "Balm in Gilead" was employed regularly by men and women as they struggled to survive the rages of slavery.

Reflecting on living conditions, the horror of the daily grind, and the traumas with which slaves were constantly faced we might find it amazing that the slaves survived at all—emotionally and physically. Indeed, slaves got weary. The conviction that slavery was an evil institution is reflected in the phrase, "Sometimes I feel discouraged." Slaves were saying, "Why go on? Why keep on working and slaving only to suffer?" Maybe the slaves, when confronted with constant abuse and degradation, also grew tired of holding on to the countercultural belief that they were worthy, good, and valuable to God. Maybe they began to believe that they were actually no better than animals or chattel.

Thousands of slave mothers watched their children, even infants, being sold away from them They never saw them again. Slave husbands and fathers were not allowed to protect their wives or their children and were just as easily sold away from their loved ones. This pain of separation, coupled with backbreaking work with no pay, little food, horrible living conditions, and the threat of physical abuse gave slaves many reasons to lament.

"She rose to her feet, and said, in piteous tones, 'My Lord and Master, help me! My load is more than I can bear. God has hid himself from me, and I am left in darkness and misery.' Then, striking her breast, she continued, 'I can't tell you what is in here! They've got all my children. Last week they took the last one. God only knows where they've sold her. They let me have her sixteen years, and then—O! O! Pray for her brothers and sisters! I've got nothing to live for now. God make my time short!' She sat down, quivering in every limb."

—Excerpt from Harriet Jacobs,
"A Piteous Prayer to a Hidden God" (1861)

Yet, we know that slaves lived on, birthed children who continued the struggle, and finally, as a people, were freed from slavery; although the trials did not end there. How did slaves survive? Why didn't they all commit suicide or simply give up and die? Where did their hope come from? What allowed them to keep going?

Slaves were not blind to the enormous pain and suffering they had to endure. Life was hard, and it showed. Many slaves managed to hold on, not just to their lives, but also to their spirits. By continuing to sing and pray at night, many slaves, led by their own preachers, clung to the hope that they would one day be free. As a slave preacher explained, "I tell them if they keep praying, the Lord will set them free." Slaves held on to their sanity through their faith in God, thus making the best out of their lives.

The testimony of the spirituals indicates that slaves were strengthened by the power of God that came from within. Although many slaves attended church with their masters, heard evangelists, and attended camp meetings and revivals, it was the testimony burning within their hearts that gave them the strength to hold on. Inspired by the gospel fundamentals to which they were exposed, slaves were able to transform and redefine their understanding of the Christian faith. The slave community appropriated religion through the teachings of Christ and the Old Testament stories, finding the true meaning of the gospel. All persons are precious and equal in God's sight. Slaves adopted a strict moral code in which they sincerely believed that if they adhered to the teachings of God's law and remained obedient to the faith, they would be rewarded in life and in heaven. They also believed that slave masters, as well as any evil person, would be judged by God. Slaves recognized that although society may be unjust, the God of mercy is not.

Although many preachers and masters tried to convince slaves that it was God's will they remain in bondage, the words of the spirituals illustrate that slaves did not believe this teaching. They comforted each other with spirituals like "Balm in Gilead," a comfort that was needed in a cruel and difficult world. This song suggests that the slaves felt that there was a better world in which they could be soothed and nurtured by God and the heavenly host. Symbolically, Gilead was the place to obtain the balm to soothe their souls, a balm of comfort and healing. Perhaps Gilead also was the spiritual center within that slaves could experience through prayer and worship.

In addition, underlying the meaning and tone of "Balm in Gilead" is the heart of social protest. Slaves believed that the world could be better. They looked forward to societal transformation, not just heavenly reward. Slaves were holding on because they believed that society could change for their children. Therefore, Gilead was not only a spiritual haven from which to receive a balm of rest, but it was also a sociopolitical goal that the slave community believed would one day be manifested. As the spiritual indicates, sometimes many slaves were discouraged; but the song says, "But then the Holy Spirit revives my soul again." It was the power within, the power of divine energy that pulsated inside and gave them new life to keep doing and being. The God inside, through the power of the Holy Spirit, reminded them they were God's children.

Jeremiah's Cry: Jeremiah 8:14-22

Jeremiah was a Hebrew prophet of the seventh and sixth centuries BC. The prominence of the prophetic voice and the overwhelming mood of despair in Jeremiah 8:14-22 have led biblical scholars to view this passage as a lament. The prophet was obviously dismayed as he reflected on Israel's political status as well as her relationship to and standing before God. He realized that Israel was facing calamity because of her sins, so he wrote under the sign of a great, impending doom. Jeremiah was trying to warn the people that they would be destroyed by God if they did not change their ways.

At issue was Israel's failure to repent before God for the images and foreign idols they had worshiped (verse 19). The season for repentance had passed, and God's anger was provoked. Thus, the peace that Israel anticipated did not come, and trouble or terror would replace the "time of healing" (verse 15) that many expected. Jeremiah used certain images or metaphors to convey a sense of the calamity that was to come. The bitterness of gall (verse 14) indicated the hard realities the people had to endure. "The snorting of his horses" (verse 16) referred to the enemy from the north that would devour the land, the city, and all that dwelled there. Some Bible commentators interpret this as a reference to the cavalry of King

Nebuchadnezzar, which was coming from Phoenicia and had already reached Dan, an area located to the extreme north of Palestine. Because of such possible destruction, and perhaps because of the impending signs of war, Israel became a nation in grief.

Equally significant is the prophet's total identification with the hardships and sorrows of the Israelites. It is clear that his pain emerged out of a deep concern for the comfort and welfare of his people. Their wounds became his wounds, and Jeremiah was tortured by his own personal, internal, and spiritual depression. He hurt for the suffering of the people. Confronted with the people's sense of panic and his own despair, Jeremiah surrendered his optimism to an emerging pessimism. He lamented his failure to find a healer for the people. Thus, he asked, "Is there no balm in Gilead? \ Is there no physician there?"

Balm of Gilead is an evergreen shrub with white blossoms that become green apple-like fruit. These plants grow in plains near the Dead Sea. The fruit is picked before it is fully ripe, and a sweet oil is taken from it. This oil is called *lukkum* in Arabic and is marketed as "Balm of Gilead." In ancient times, value was found in the bark of the plant because its gum resin gave a fragrance that was an ingredient for medicine.

Gilead was a highland region located beyond Jordan and on the eastern horizion. It was among the Israelite territories that fell to the enemy during Jeremiah's time. Gilead was the place where one found the trees, herbs, and flowers to make the balsams that supplied the physicians of the eastern world. Indeed, many physicians resided in this city because of the easy supply of medicines; and people would travel from all over for medical attention. Gilead was like one great hospital. And yet, Gilead was more than a geographical setting. It also symbolized hope and comfort. Jeremiah asked, "Is there no balm in Gilead? \ Is there no physician there?"

Because of Jeremiah's pessimism and despair, the answer in the context of his query is a categorical no. There was no physician, prophet, or remedy left that could heal wounded hearts, give hope to the hopeless, and comfort the afflicted. In expressing his negative mood, Jeremiah used the words *harvest* and *summer* to explain that the time of joy was no more. He wrote, "The harvest is passed, the summer is ended, \ and we are not saved." Symbolically, the words *harvest* and *summer* also refer to the time of gathering in the planted crop, which happened in the fall. Jeremiah was saying they had gathered the crops, but the yield did not provide the necessary balm to heal the people.

The Slaves' Answer: There Is a Balm

The spiritual "Balm in Gilead" is a testimony to the powerful faith and hope on the part of the slaves. In the midst of their oppressive surroundings, conditions that could not have been worse than the difficulties experienced by the prophet Jeremiah and the Israelites, the slaves managed to offer an affirmative reply to Jeremiah's question, "Is there no balm in Gilead? \ Is there no physician there?" The slaves understood Jeremiah's question to be essentially a question about his struggles, and they identified with him and the pain of the Israelites. They responded, "*Yes*, there is a balm in Gilead," indicating that in the midst of their afflictions they believed that comfort did exist and would come.

"Balm in Gilead" becomes an excellent illustration of how pain and joy could exist side by side in the lives of the slaves. While suffering and sorrow marked their existence, the slaves still had hope. They had hope for a better way of life for this world and for a better existence in the world to come. Slaves believed that all their wounds would be healed because the balm in Gilead was embodied in the person and sacrifice of Jesus Christ, who endured an atoning and redemptive death on the cross.

Carrying the Balm's Mantle

As Christians we often face our share of difficulties and problems. "Balm in Gilead," composed from the scriptural context of Jeremiah 8:14-22, has much to teach anyone striving to develop a stronger, faith-filled relationship with God. Understanding the circumstances out of which the slaves developed this spiritual can serve as an inspiration to us as we encounter tribulations. When singing this spiritual, slaves often closed their eyes and imagined the Spirit of the Lord embracing them with loving arms, comforting them as if rubbing a soothing balm across their souls. Whether in private meditation, prayer groups, or camp meetings, singing this spiritual became a holy ritual for slaves in times of suffering, loneliness, and oppression. When this spiritual was introduced by slaves to their masters, "Balm in Gilead" quickly became popular in white churches and revivals across the country. The beautiful melody of the song, coupled with the rich meaning of the words, continues to resonate with Christians the world over.

The religious heritage of the African American church and community, which sustained the mantle of hope and determination from the slaves, also serves to remind us that there is healing and comfort in the midst of our many afflictions. This conviction has been embodied in African American leaders, pastors, and lay persons who have striven to encourage and care for hurting persons, even as they urged society to turn away from economic

inequalities, unfair judicial treatment, labor discrimination, and other preju-
dicial behavior perpetuated against minorities. Today, many continue to rec-
ognize that some of the same concerns found in the prophetic tradition of
Jeremiah are echoed in contemporary society in the forms of racism, mili-
tarism, and the mistreatment of the poor and the oppressed. We are all called
as children of God to stand for the people, even as Jeremiah did. The
prophet's example teaches us to strive to help the needy and the downtrod-
den of our communities, even as we reach for the love and comfort of God
in our own sorrows.

FOOD FOR THOUGHT

1. Compare and contrast the mood reflected in Jeremiah's question "Is
   there no balm in Gilead?" with that of the spiritual "Balm in
   Gilead." Is Jeremiah's question applicable to the slaves' situation?
   What do the words and mood of the song indicate about the slaves'
   beliefs about suffering and healing? How is Jeremiah's question rel-
   evant today? What is a contemporary view of healing and suffering?

2. What are some of the images and metaphors that Jeremiah uses to
   express both his own personal pain and sorrow and that of the people of Israel? Are these images and metaphors useful for African
   Americans and other peoples today? How so?

3. Why is Jeremiah considered a prophet? Is it proper to say that
   African American church leaders have long stood in the prophetic
   tradition shaped by Jeremiah and other ancient Hebrews? Why or
   why not?

4. What is the role of the contemporary prophet? Is he or she called to
   comfort the afflicted, or to afflict the comfortable? Is there a need for
   churches to recapture the prophetic heritage of the Bible? What sort
   of "balm" is needed for the contemporary Christian church? How do
   we as Christians stand in this spiritual tradition? In what ways do we
   need to recapture it?

Session Four

Mark 8:34-35

Key verse: "For those who want to save their life will lose it, and those who lose their life for my sake, and for the sake of the gospel, will save it" (Mark 8:35).

"Ain't Dat Good News?"

Verse:
Got a crown up in-a dat Kingdom,
Ain't-a dat good news?
Got a crown up in-a dat Kingdom.
Ain't-a dat good news?

Got a harp up in-a dat Kingdom...
(Repeat Chorus)
Got a robe up in-a dat Kingdom...
(Repeat Chorus)

Chorus:
I'm a-gonna lay down dis world,
Gonna shoulder up my cross,
Gonna take it home-a to my Jesus,
Ain't-a dat good news?

Verse:
Got slippers in-a dat Kingdom...
(Repeat Chorus)
Got a Savior in-a dat Kingdom...
(Repeat Chorus)

Joyous Musical Expression

"Ain't Dat Good News" is quick in tempo and spirited and lively in expression. Its rhythm is punctuated by a strong, steady beat. Singers and hearers alike share the experience of moving along from accent to accent almost in a rush throughout the entire song. Soft notes, subtle tones, and a quick pace, along with the song's message, convey a sense of urgency. A hurried restlessness can also be heard in the timbre and style of the male and female voices. There is a quiet but determined edge to each voice blended together in harmony. The impression of happiness and excitement is created as the song travels from verse to verse, seemingly focused on reaching the end. As the rich and

27

> "[Slaves] went up [the river] to other plantations [to] dances [and all those] things, [and they were] awful fond [of singing] songs. [The] grown folkses [would sing and] somebody would pick [the] banjo."
>
> —Alice Baugh, former slave, 1937

tranquil voices glide along the melody, the harmonies sound effortless and natural.

Mighty Good News

"Ain't Dat Good News" was sung by slaves in various settings. It was sung also by freedom fighters during the Civil Rights Movement in the 1960s. With its upbeat tempo and inspirational theme, "Ain't Dat Good News" is motivational and encouraging. During slavery, the song helped to inspire many African Americans to entertain visions of salvation and freedom. Slaves confronted the endless burden of hard work and desperate living conditions with the belief that there really was good news.

> "With so few possessions to call their own, and scant prospects of wealth in any degree, the biblical promise of a crown, etc. in the kingdom made an intolerable situation more tolerable. This song is unrestrained joy! Going home to be with Jesus had no downside: It was all good news. Its spirited tempo and easy-to-follow melody make "Ain't Dat Good News" suitable for an anthem, special choral selection, or concert rendition."
>
> ——William B. McClain
> *Come Sunday: The Liturgy of Zion* (1990)

Because of the soft, yet lively, tone and flow of the song, we can imagine a group of slaves huddled in a corner next to a horse shed or behind a work cabin, chanting in low tones the beautiful melodies of this spiritual. The tempo remains upbeat throughout with a vibrant, strong style. It seems the words to the song had to be expressed quickly, because the group may have had to scatter if the master or overseer came. Perhaps the slaves sang with the threat of being punished if caught. Yet, they continued to sing hurriedly and with purpose. They believed the good news had to be shared. The singers may have laughed softly, filled with hope at the joy that awaited them in heaven as they gently clapped their hands or patted their feet to the rhythm. Almost like adventurers, the group may have participated in this secret activity with relish. Their communal solidarity was expressed in the telling of God's good news to each other through song.

Since the song is expressing good news, slaves happily sang to each other the promise of the crown, the harp, the robe, and the slippers they expected to wear in God's kingdom because of their dire earthly conditions. Like other

> "My dress was usually split from hem to neck and I had to wear them till they was strings. [I went] barefoot summer and winter till the feets crack."
>
> —Tempie Cummins, ex-slave, 1938

spirituals, the inclusion of these verses in "Ain't Dat Good News" reflects a protest of the living conditions slaves were forced to endure. In God's kingdom—in heaven and on earth—wrongs would be righted; and all God's children would have shoes, clothing, a crown, and even a harp. In the Kingdom, the inequities and injustices of the world would be fixed. The slaves, walking barefoot on the cold, hard road or suffering freezing cold or blistering heat, could gather and remind each other quietly that even though things might have been rough and terrible at the moment, trouble would not last always.

In another setting almost one hundred years later, the descendants of slaves, along with men and women of all races, marched together amidst the threat of physical harm and death. During the 1960s in the South, the group was looking ahead to another kind of freedom: full acceptance and equality in society for all persons. On dusty, hot Southern roads, singers walked together step by step chanting the melodies of their ancestors. They were empowered by the vitality and exuberance of "Ain't Dat Good News." The sun burned down on their backs, and hecklers teased them from the roadside. They were cursed and spat upon. Police dogs and chains threatened their bodies, and ragtag mobs in old pickup trucks attempted to run them over. Still they continued to sing, marching to the beat of the song, believing fervently in the good news, the hope that God wanted a better life for their families and their community.

Jesus' Testimony: Mark 8:34-36

In this text, Jesus speaks to the people and his disciples about the meaning of salvation. In order to be saved, they must deny the self while taking up the cross and following him. Although this task will not be easy, Jesus provides the ultimate example by taking up his own cross and dying for the sins of the people. By word and deed, Jesus indicated that nothing in the material world and the earthly life can measure up to the inner person or the

29

soul. This inner person, found within every individual, has the opportunity to have an everlasting relationship with God. This is the good news, the gospel. There is a life that is not sought in the world but in the Spirit, which is God. To attain everlasting life, we must follow Christ instead of worldly temptations, entrusting heart, mind, and soul to God.

Crowns in the Kingdom

From hearing Bible stories in church with their masters, in secret worship services with other slaves, or in learning to read Scripture, slaves adapted the message of the good news to their understanding of God, life, and heaven. Slaves believed that although their physical lives were tormented and burdened, they would one day "lay down this world." Jesus stated, "For those who want to save their life will lose it, and those who lose their life for my sake, and for the sake of the gospel, will save it" (Mark 8:35). By giving up worldly desires and pursuits and turning completely to Christ in obedience to God's will, the soul is saved by grace. The slaves stated this emphatically by singing, "Gonna lay down this world," indicating that they were accepting Jesus' offer. By choosing not to attempt to gain the world and therefore lose their lives, the slaves chose instead to place their hopes on life in Christ. Like Jesus, the slaves could shoulder up the cross of this world, the cross of affliction, and achieve the peace and assurance of a life with God. Such a proposition gave them an enormous amount of hope. Moreover, having something to look forward to beyond this world was extremely encouraging. Not only could slaves struggle to survive with the power of God in their hearts, they had an eternal reward to look forward to. The belief in the good news encouraged thousands of slaves to believe that things could get better. Slaves were able to pass the spirit of freedom and hope as a legacy to succeeding generations.

The assurance in the words and tone of "Ain't Dat Good News" demonstrates that the slaves believed that a good life was waiting for them. The crown was already in the kingdom, as well as the harp, the robe, and the slippers. Their place was already set; their space was already reserved. This was the good news. The urgency of "Ain't Dat Good News" expressed in the lively tempo and steady rhythm creates the sense that the slaves believed it would not be long before they could "lay down this world." Slaves believed that the world of their servitude would one day end, and they would experience freedom. Indeed, that belief is reflected in the urgency that builds from verse to verse. By using the rhetorical device of describing what would be waiting for them in the Kingdom, the slaves created momentum of excitement and hopefulness.

"What, though I mourn and am afflicted here, and sigh under the miseries of this world for a time, I am sure that my tears shall one day be turned into joy, and that joy none shall take from me. Whoever hopes for the great things in this world, takes pains to attain them; how can my hopes of everlasting life be well grounded, if I do not strive and labor for that eternal inheritance?"

—A.M.E. Bishop and Founder Richard Allen, "A Prayer for Hope," (1787-1830)

Further, the strong conviction of the verses, which declare with authority that the rewards are waiting for the believers in heaven and would one day be available to believers on earth, shows that the slaves had assurance. They were convinced that they were saved by God's grace, that they were true followers of Jesus. The tone of celebration in the spiritual makes clear that the slaves believed the good news applied to them. By "shouldering up the cross," slaves were testifying to their faithful service and obedience. The slaves were not going to be left out but had a definite place in the Kingdom. Here, the Kingdom is not only heaven, as was expected, but the Kingdom anywhere the Spirit of God had reign. By singing this song, the slaves were ushering in the kingdom of God, confronting the evil of the world through the power of God and their fervent belief in that power.

Taking Up Our Crosses

We, like the slaves, have the opportunity to increase our understanding of what it means to take up our crosses and follow Jesus. What does it mean for us to "lay down this world"? Clearly we are called to be obedient and faithful to God; but can we say that the example of Christians today indicates a readiness to take up the cross for the gospel of Christ? Are we as assured as the slaves were about everlasting life and the presence of God in our lives? Are we as fearless and motivated by the gospel as were the freedom marchers of the 1960's and other persons throughout history who stood for the cause of Christ, even at the threat of death?

Many Christian leaders have been willing to go to jail, suffer verbal and physical abuse, and even face assassination because of their devotion to the gospel. Others have suffered exile from their countries, endured starvation and torture, and have been rejected by family and community because they refused to put their own needs and desires above the calling to follow Christ. This kind of sacrifice reflects Jesus' own example and call to others to take up one's cross and live for God. Living constantly under the shadow of degradation, oppression, and death, the slaves recognized this Christian truth by composing the beautiful spiritual "Ain't Dat Good News." What are we doing to usher in God's kingdom? What is our testimony?

FOOD FOR THOUGHT

1. **What was Jesus' definition of the good news? Did African American slaves have this same understanding? Would you say the spiritual "Ain't Dat Good News" conveys essentially the same meaning as Mark 8:34-35? Why or why not? Are some themes enlarged? Are there other elements in the passage that are missing in the spiritual?**

2. **What is the kingdom of God? What is the slaves' interpretation as reflected in the spiritual? Is this consistent with Jesus' descriptions? What is the relationship between worldly and otherworldly concerns in "Ain't Dat Good News"?**

3. **What did the crown, the slippers, the harp, and the Savior mean for the slaves? Do they have the same meaning for us today? Do we think of different images when we reflect on heaven and the kingdom of God? What do you think about the statement that, due to the conditions of their lives, some people today are already living in heaven while others are living in hell?**

4. **What did Jesus mean when he told his disciples to take up their crosses? How should we interpret this in contemporary life? What is your definition of sacrificial leadership? How can we tell when we must accept the circumstances causing us pain or trouble? When must we work to change those circumstances? Do expectations of relief and justice in heaven mean that we do not invest ourselves in righting the wrongs in society that we see?**

Session Five

Acts 2:1-4

Key verse: "All of them were filled with the Holy Spirit and began to speak in other languages, as the Spirit gave them ability" (Acts 2:4).

"Every Time I Feel the Spirit"

Chorus:
Every time I feel the Spirit
Moving in my heart, I will pray.
Yes, every time I feel the Spirit
Moving in my heart, I will pray.

Verse:
Upon the mountain my Lord spoke,
Out of His mouth came fire and smoke.
Looked all around me, it looked so shine,
Till I asked my Lord if all was mine.

Every time I feel the Spirit
Moving in my heart, I will pray.
Yes, every time I feel the Spirit
Moving in my heart, I will pray.

Verse:
Jordan River is chilly and cold,
It chills the body but not the soul.
There ain't but one train on this track,
Runs to heaven and right back.
(Repeat Chorus)

Lively Celebration

"Every Time I Feel the Spirit" is extremely lively and dramatic in style. This celebratory feel coats the flow and melody of the song. Singers' voices run up and down the musical scale in order to capture all the notes of this vivacious spiritual. An appreciative proclamation is delivered by the voices, for this is a wonderful, exciting time: the experience of the Holy Spirit! Rhythmic and pulsating, accents adorn each word, with an emphasis on *every, time, feel, moving,* and *pray.* The bass voice pauses for a more solemn and descriptive tone during the verses with warm and well-spaced tones. Then all the voices rush back to the chorus with the original lively beat. It is

> During the Civil War, a slave named Aunt Mary Dives, a cook in the White House, helped to keep "Every Time I Feel the Spirit" alive. When Aunt Mary led in the singing of this spiritual at the White House, President Abraham would find himself joining in, bowing his head, or wiping tears from his face.
>
> — John Lovell, *Black Song: The Forge and the Flame* (1972)

as if while singing the verses the bass has an important story to convey and therefore slows down the rhythm and colors the tones to sound more authoritative.

By the time the chorus is repeated, there is a sense of familiarity with the melody and harmony in the rest of the voices and a seeming expectation that listeners will want to join in the singing. "Every Time I Feel the Spirit" is expressive, happy, and festive.

Prayer and Slavery

"Every Time I Feel the Spirit" indicates the importance of prayer and the Holy Spirit to the slaves. In their understanding, one could not really sing or worship without feeling the Spirit. Integral to life was the omnipresence of God in the form of the Holy Spirit. Without it there was no heart, no joy, no depth in living. An ex-slave named Sarah Ashley explained: "I took the white children to church sometimes, but they couldn't teach me to sing because I didn't have any Spirit." To the slaves it was impossible to sing and worship without the Spirit. It simply was not done. This belief was a carryover from an African worldview, the ancestral legacy of the slaves. The African worldview affirmed the sacred world as thoroughly enmeshed and central to all aspects of life. God was everywhere and experienced in all things. Singing was simply another act involving the Divine, so it was impossible to sing or worship without the holy presence.

> "Thou hast made us for thyself, and our souls are restless till they find rest in thee."
>
> —Saint Augustine, North Africa (354-430 A.D.)

Without the presence of the Holy Spirit, songs were empty and meaningless. From numerous recorded testimonies of ex-slaves, it is clear that they constantly prayed for freedom, not only at prayer meetings, but also throughout the day while working in the fields or cooking in the kitchens. Slaves believed in the power of prayer and included it in their daily lives.

A SLAVE FATHER'S PRAYER

"When the time came for us to go to bed we all knelt down in family prayer, as was our custom; father's prayer seemed more real to me that night than ever before, especially in the words, 'Lord, hasten the time when these children shall be their own free men and women.'

My faith in my father's prayer made me think that the Lord would answer him at the fartherest in two or three weeks, but it was fully six years before it came, and father had been dead two years before the war."

—Jacob Stroyer (1898)

The act of prayer lessened the distance between the human soul and God. Those who prayed, whether individually or in groups, opened up heart and soul to Jesus, focusing entirely on divine energy. Borrowed from the African past of ritual and ceremony, the praying moment was sacred; and through it the presence and power of God could be ushered in and felt by all those around. Slaves expected miracles and prayed accordingly. Call-and-response, effective through music and preaching, was also experienced in prayer. When a leader prayed, the group would respond in the affirmative; thus praying was a communal act. As the speaker prayed one line, others would answer "Yes, Lord,"

CALL-AND-RESPONSE PRAYER

We are here this evening, Jesus
  Oh yeah
We can't do nothing without you
  Uh huh
Come Holy Spirit, Heavenly Dove
  Oh yeah
With all thou quickening power
  Power!
Kindle the flame of our Savior's love
  Yeah!
In these cold hearts of ours!

—James Brown,
"You Know the Purpose of Our Gathering, Jesus" (1980)

> "But if I could be [the] whole judge of [the] whole world, I think [the] best thing would be for people to be on [their] knees... prayin.' "
>
> —Liney Henderson, ex-slave, 1938

or "Thank You, Jesus." The speaker would follow with another line, and the group would reply. This pattern would be repeated throughout the prayer.

Slaves believed literally that where two or three were gathered together in Jesus' name, the power of the Holy Spirit would come and dwell among them. This Spirit could be experienced directly, as when the rush of holy power would come upon one's own being. Lifted up in joy and release, one could get "happy." By becoming full of the Spirit, a worshiper experienced the urge to testify, jump, shout, run, or even dance.

Exhilaration at experiencing the unconditional and overwhelming love of God, manifest as a forgiving, healing, and transforming divine affection, was so meaningful to slaves that late-night prayer meetings would some-times last all night. Release from the spiritual and psychological trauma of the daily grind of slavery was accomplished through the power of prayer. Appreciation for the powerful effects of prayer in their lives through the power of the Holy Spirit must have inspired the original singers to compose "Every Time I Feel the Spirit."

The verses of "Every Time I Feel the Spirit" indicate Hebrew Bible ref-erences. "Upon the mountain, my Lord spoke" recalls the meeting of Moses and God along with the delivered people of Israel at Mount Sinai. Such a pronouncement of the presence of God on the mountain demonstrates the power and authority of God. Slaves were calling on the mighty being of God who is stronger than any human, master or otherwise. This God was appar-ent in the Holy Spirit and offered the Spirit to anyone who was able to receive it. Slaves were just as able as masters to receive the presence of the Holy Spirit.

The second verse, "Jordan River is chilly and cold," also evokes the pas-sage of the Israelites crossing the Jordan River; but it also refers to the sacra-ment of baptism. Here, the warmth and love of God experienced through the regenerating act of baptism counteracts the physical temperature of water.

The Holy Spirit Comes: Acts 2:1-4

The Acts of the Apostles records the birth of an early Christian commu-nity created by the coming of the Holy Spirit upon the band of believers who had followed Jesus' earthly ministry. The presence of the Holy Spirit was overt and dramatic; according to the words of the text, the Spirit came as the "rush of a violent wind." Each person present was filled with power from God; tongues of fire rested on every one of the believers; and they were given amazing abilities.

The second part of the first verse, "all around me, looked so shine," reflects directly on the light from the tongues of fire on the people, the glory of the Holy Spirit. The supernatural gift of speaking other languages was a sign of the awesome majesty of God as revealed in the Spirit. The people in the upper room were lifted up and transformed from their ordinary selves into powerful witnesses for Christ. The glorious speech coming from their mouths, decipherable by those from other lands, told of the saving grace and unconditional love of Jesus Christ. They were proclaiming the message of God's deliverance that was available to all who heard and believed.

The Spirit was living and active, moving through souls in order to invigorate, to heal, and to restore them. This dramatic event, recorded for all posterity, illustrates the remarkable workings of the magnificent Holy Spirit, presenting to all Christians descriptive characteristics of what the Spirit is like. Clearly, the Holy Spirit is wonderful, incomprehensible, and earth-shattering!

Pentecost as Empowerment

The Pentecost experience, as reflected in Acts, has had an enduring influence on African American churches through the legacy of slave theology. Some contemporary scholars believe that the Pentecost experience as described in the Bible offers the best missional and evangelizing tool for the renewal and revitalization of the Christian church through the world.

Pentecost reminds us that our churches must always be in renewal under the power of the Holy Spirit. Pentecost represents an indwelling of God's Spirit. The Spirit is alive, fresh, and positive. It is full of life and bequeaths life to all persons through God. Indeed, the experience of the Spirit, which was evident in "Every Time I Feel the Spirit" and passed on through generations, is simply a taste of the awesome power that heaven has to offer. The Holy Spirit gives us a glimpse of how wonderful it will be to live forever with God while transforming the experience of two or three gathered together in the Lord's name.

By learning about the experiences of the slaves, we can be inspired to encounter the Spirit anew in our lives. Although our personal and communal situations may vary, we too deal with various problems and pain in our lives. In reflecting on the slaves' testimonies and singing their words, we can turn to God through the power of the Spirit to be renewed and empowered.

FOOD FOR THOUGHT

1. Reflect on your personal knowledge and understanding of the experience of the slaves in America. Does the fact that they were able to compose such a beautiful, uplifting spiritual, despite the condition of their lives, offer a testimony to you about the power of the Holy Spirit? How do you think it is possible for people to have strong faith in the midst of oppression?

2. Briefly describe the significance of the Pentecost experience in Acts 2. What did Pentecost mean for African American slaves as echoed in "Every Time I Feel the Spirit"?

3. What did the Spirit mean to the slaves? How did they incorporate an understanding of the Holy Spirit into their daily lives? Were they sensitive to feeling the presence of God? How is this presence apparent in contemporary worship? When have you experienced a sudden awareness of the Spirit of God? How might we learn to be more open to seeing the Spirit at work?

4. How were the people in Acts 2 transformed by the power of the Holy Spirit? How can we pass on the importance of a spiritual like "Every Time I Feel the Spirit" to future generations? What can we do to preserve our history in the minds of people? Is it accurate to conclude that to understand where a people and a nation have come from is to understand where that people and nation are going?

Session Six

John 14:1-4

Key verse: "In my Father's house there are many dwelling places. If it were not so, would I have told you that I go to prepare a place for you?" (John 14:2).

"Plenty Good Room"

Chorus:
There's plenty good room, plenty good room,
Plenty good room in my Father's kingdom,
Plenty good room, plenty good room,
Just choose your seat and sit down!

Verse:
I would not be a sinner,
I'll tell you the reason why;
I'm afraid my Lord might call on me,
And I wouldn't be ready to die.

There's plenty good room, plenty good room,
Plenty good room in my Father's kingdom,
Plenty good room, plenty good room,
Just choose your seat and sit down!

Verse:
I would not be a liar,
I'll tell you the reason why;
I'm afraid my Lord might call on me,
And I wouldn't be ready to die. (Repeat Chorus)
Sit down! Sit down! Sit down!

Heaven Is a Place

"Plenty Good Room," with its spaced, unfaltering meter, allows voices in unison to expand and contract with feeling, promoting musical expression and communication of the story that all people are included in God's kingdom. This light but pronounced style gets the word across. With precise diction and round vocal phrases, the message is artfully conveyed that in heaven, as well as on earth, God's will is that there must be plenty good room. A relatively fast tempo distinguishes the chorus from the verses, which slow down and allow the tenor to explain why he "would not be a sinner" or "a liar." Harmonic

> "Heaven was a place—it was not merely an idea in the mind. This must be held in mind, constantly. The thinking about it is spatial. It is the thinking of Jesus in the Fourth Gospel.... 'In my father's house are many mansions.' "
>
> —Howard Thurman,
> *Deep River and the Negro Spiritual Speaks of Life and Death* (1975)

background singers complement the lead voice. These male and female voices, denoted by "hmmm," are simply agreeing that it is best to live right in order to get to the Kingdom. The positive, crisp color of the voices also illustrates that the room in the Kingdom, waiting for all those who follow Christ, is a comfortable and secure dwelling. The confident voices seem to be saying, "You know, there is so much room up there in God's kingdom, I can't wait to get there. You can get there, too."

The singers seem to be smiling as they sing, injecting much warmth into their delivery. The Kingdom is open to all those who love the Father, and everyone has a seat. The last line of the chorus, "Sit down, sit down, sit down!" is invitational and beckoning, giving the listener the opportunity to get a good seat. A sense of imperative urgency is also expressed as if to suggest, "Don't be silly and miss out on your chance. This is some great stuff!"

Judgment and Death

"Plenty Good Room" expresses the hopes and aspirations of slaves on many levels. Some understood that it was likely that their lives on earth would only be filled with toil and suffering. Many looked forward to life after death. Since slaves believed in an afterlife, they were convinced that

> "[The] grave and ... resurrection will put everything all right, but I have a instinct [that] God'll make it all right over and up yonder and [that] all our 'fflictions will, in [the] long run, turn out to our [eternal] welfare and happiness."
>
> —Manda Walker,
> ex-slave, 1937

the God of justice settles all accounts in heaven by punishing sinners and setting the captives free. There would be no exceptions, and all would be held accountable. It was the sincere conviction of slaves that their masters, along with all other evildoers, would be punished in the afterlife. In "Plenty Good Room" the verses stress that the Kingdom belongs to "my" father. Even though slaves knew that they were considered to be less than human in society and were mistreated, mishandled, exploited, and afflicted, they did not believe such treatment revealed their inherent worth. Slaves believed they were God's children and heirs to the kingdom. As heirs they expected to receive the inheritance promised to them by God.

While overtly referring to anticipated blessings in heaven, "Plenty Good Room" also had another message. Slaves were protesting their status in life where they were not given room to live, work, and exist as human beings. This state, as the words to the song clearly indicate, is not reflective of God's kingdom. In their "Father's kingdom" they had "plenty good room." The words of the spiritual were also a subtle protest against the tiny, one-room shacks and other deplorable lodgings in which the slaves were forced to live. Understandably, slaves longed for a place where they could have their basic physical needs met. As slaves, they physically and figuratively had no room.

Succeeding generations of African Americans extended their understanding of "Plenty Good Room" to include the equal participation of all persons at every level of society. African Americans were not given "room" to vote, work, shop, travel, or even eat equitably in the United States. Treated as members of the lower caste, they were systemically excluded from fully participating in societal life, even though they were citizens. The brutal victimization and disenfranchisement of blacks gave reason for many to despair. Spirituals like "Plenty Good Room," holy relics from the past, were dusted off and became reinvigorated symbols of the ongoing quest for human equality, even as the spiritual hope of the world beyond was maintained. This kind of activity characterized the Civil Rights Movement of the 1950s and 1960s.

> "Plenty Good Room" became internationally popular around the world through concert performances by singing groups like the Fisk Jubliee Singers of Tennessee and the Hampton University Singers of Virginia.

Mansions in the Sky: John 14:1-4

Jesus told his disciples that he was preparing them for his upcoming arrest, torture, and crucifixion. Although the disciples may not have been fully aware of it, Jesus knew that they would all experience much suffering and tribulation. To strengthen them for the difficult road ahead, he offered them comfort. Despite the fact that they would face horrible afflictions and troubles, outrage, and despair, Jesus promised them a final victory. He knew

41

> "I'll just wait on here, and [the] waitin' won't be much longer, 'cause I'm [living] right, an' praise the Lawd, [I'm going to heaven when] I die."
>
> —John Hill, ex-slave, 1938

that the world would seem to threaten to crash down on their heads; but his words indicate that God had already ordained the end in which his followers would succeed.

The disciples were told to hold on, even when they wanted to give in. Jesus promised that although he may be taken from them, the presence of God would never leave. Moreover, Jesus had to be taken from them so that he could go and prepare a place for all those who follow his path. Because of the disciples' love, faith, and devotion, Jesus would go to be with the Father and prepare a place. He revealed that "there are many mansions" in God's house. Jesus, the divine carpenter, was going to design dwelling places for all of eternity for his disciples. There they would be at rest and at peace with God always. "So do not fret," Jesus said. "I will not leave you alone. I will not abandon you." As children of the Father, the disciples were entitled to live with Jesus forever.

Standing on the Shoulders of Giants

From "Plenty Good Room" and its biblical references, we know that the slaves readily identified with the disciples' situation in the Gospel of John. The disciples had already suffered a great deal to follow Christ, and soon they would suffer much more. Like the disciples, the slaves were filled with sadness and grief. They felt as if they were far away from Jesus, living in a world of toil and strain. However, they were empowered by Jesus' message to them that a better place awaits. As fellow suffering Christians, the slaves appropriated the message Jesus gave the disciples and identified with the divine hope. The slaves held on to the belief that if they trusted in Jesus and held on to the faith, they would one day live with Jesus in one of heaven's glorious mansions. And yet even before that time, like the disciples, the slaves resolved to follow Jesus, serving God fully in spirit and truth. In this way, slaves stood on the shoulders of their faithful forbears, the disciples in the text, who managed to hold on to the faith and become witnesses for Christ.

Our Calling

We still have the opportunity to stand on the shoulders of giants. The Christian slaves, especially those who composed, sang, and passed down the spirituals, are ancestors of all Christians striving to live faithfully according to the teachings of Jesus Christ. Today we face challenges different from those of previous generations. Millions of people are refugees, cut off from their own homelands. Others, such as homeless persons in the United States, are neglected and treated like aliens in their own countries. Unwanted immigrants struggle with the need for acceptance and affirmation from one side of the globe to the other. Millions of people are simply struggling to survive.

Indeed the human struggle for a sense of belonging is at the core of territorial disputes, terrorist attacks, and wars. Oppressive economic and political systems help to incur anger and hatred among groups, sparking violence and destruction. Even in less socially disturbed surroundings, many individuals struggle with severe inner turmoil. There may be family or childhood abuse in the home, birthing rage and psychosis. Some people become suicidal and homicidal, engaging in dangerous behaviors such as drug abuse, sexual misconduct, and other harmful outlets.

"Plenty Good Room" represents the abundance of blessings that God has in store for us. How do we incorporate this understanding of vast love, mercy, and inclusion for all in the practical ways we confront societal and personal ills? God promises to be lavish in generous spiritual blessings for those who are obedient. We, like the slaves and others before us, have much for which to be hopeful. If we open ourselves completely to the overriding grace of God, the possibilities are endless. An amazing realization is that God, the Creator of a limitless universe, wants to share this universe with us! Our task is to work to mature spiritually in order to discover better solutions for our lives.

"O God of love, Power and Justice.... Make compassion and the spirit of sacrifice to be the new mark of affluence of character. Strengthen us to face reality and to withstand the rigor of tough times in the anticipation of a bright side beyond the struggle. Inspire, empower, and sustain us until we reach the mountaintop, and see that future for which our hearts yearn."

—James Forbes, "O God of Love, Power, and Justice" (1990)

The prospect of righteous suffering is daunting to many. Like the disciples, we may chafe at the thought of having to endure trials in order to become stronger in our faith and get closer to God. We may want to run away from God in an attempt to avoid the cost of discipleship. Yet we have saints upon whom to reflect: those oppressed with overwhelming odds and steeped in the mires of hurt. These steadfast men and women were still able to foresee the brighter day God had in store for them. We must remain ever diligent in pressing forward, holding fast to the promise that "there is plenty good room in my Father's kingdom." The morning looms ahead, though we may be basking in the tears of night. As God's children we are yet convinced of the reward.

FOOD FOR THOUGHT

1. "Plenty Good Room" describes a view of heaven held by many slaves. Describe your view of heaven. Is it similar to or different from the image expressed in "Plenty Good Room"? How does the image of heaven in this song influence our view of heaven today?

2. What images does "Plenty Good Room" evoke in the context of living in the here and now? What is the abundant life? What are some of the ways that a stronger relationship with Christ can be nurtured that will lead to the abundant life?

3. Is the slaves' emphasis on the afterlife a helpful way to develop a faithful strategy for living in the here and now? Does focusing on heaven affect the way you hope or look forward to events in this life?

4. What is the contemporary view of suffering and martyrdom for the Christian faith? How can today's Christians develop a sacrificial interpretation of what it means to follow Christ?

References

Confessions of Saint Augustine, by Augustine (Image Books, 1960).

"You Know the Purpose of Our Gathering, Jesus," by James Brown in *Conversations With God: Two Centuries of Prayers by African Americans.* Melvin Washington, editor (HarperCollins, 1994).

Born in Slavery: Slave Narratives From the Federal Writers' Project, 1936-38 (Manuscript Division, Library of Congress).

Songs of Zion, J. Jefferson Cleveland, editor (Abingdon Press, 1981, 1982).

The Spirituals and the Blues, by James H. Cone (Seabury Press, 1972).

"Prayers From a Pilgrim's Journal," by Daniel Coker in *Journal of Daniel Coker, a Descendant of Africa* (Edward J. Coale, 1820).

"O God of Love, Power, and Justice," by James Alexander Forbes, Jr. in *Conversations With God: Two Centuries of Prayers by African Americans* (HarperCollins, 1994).

Africanisms in American Culture, by Joseph E. Holloway (Indiana University Press, 1991).

"A Piteous Prayer to a Hidden God," by Harriet A. Jacobs in *Incidents in the Life of a Slave Girl Written by Herself.* Jean Fagan Yellin, editor, (Harvard University Press, 1987 revised edition).

Wade in the Water: The Wisdom of the Spirituals, by Arthur C. Jones and Vincent Harding (Orbis Books, 1993).

Exorcising Evil: A Womanist Perspective on the Spirituals, by Cheryl Kirk-Duggan (Orbis Books, 1997).

Black Song: The Forge and the Flame: The Story of How the Afro-American Spiritual Was Hammered Out, by John Lovell, Jr. (Macmillan, 1972).

Come Sunday, The Liturgy of Zion: A Companion to Songs of Zion, by William B. McClain (Abingdon Press, 1990).

"A Slave Father's Prayer," by Jacob Stroyer in *My Life in the South* (Newcomb & Gauss, 1898).

Deep River and the Negro Spiritual Speaks of Life and Death, by Howard Thurman (Friends United Press, 1975).

Folk Songs of the American Negro, by John Wesley Work (Greenwood Publishing, 1974).